C0-DAO-517

CD Included

Requires Windows 95 or Mac 8.6 or higher

Winter Whimsy

Creative Clip Art for Classroom & Home

Created & Designed by Dianne J. Hook

ISBN 1-59441-309-6

Contents

Credits

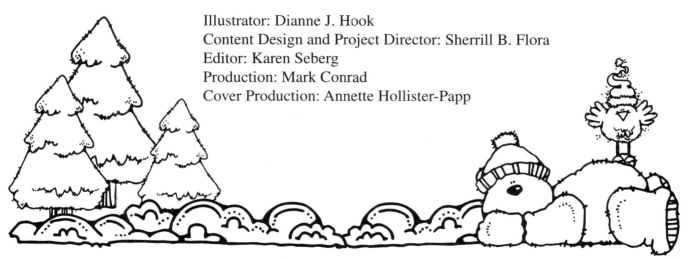

Illustrator: Dianne J. Hook
Content Design and Project Director: Sherrill B. Flora
Editor: Karen Seberg
Production: Mark Conrad
Cover Production: Annette Hollister-Papp

Clip Art Assembly Basics

Here are some suggestions as you make your flyers, announcements, or any project using clip art from this book.

Tools

Putting together the right tools will make your project go more smoothly and look better in the end. A good copy machine is a must. It's worth the extra effort to make sure your school or copy shop has machines that make clean copies. You will also need a bottle of white paper correction fluid, a fine-tip black marker to combine designs and add your own art to the project, rubber cement to mount the design on paper during the layout stage of your project, and scissors for cutting apart the designs you choose. Optional tools to help create a professional-looking project are a nonreproducible blue pencil to make marks that will not show up on copies, a proportion scale to help you determine the size of the reduction or enlargement necessary to fit your paper, and blue grid paper for laying out the project with straight lines.

Assembly Steps

1. Choose the design or designs you will be putting together for the project that you will be making.

2. Copy the design once from the book so that you have a copy from which to work without having to cut apart your book.

3. Cut out the designs from your copy and lay them out on your paper. (Blue grid paper comes in handy.) A light table can also help with the layout of your page.

4. Next, make a copy of the designs and any text on the paper before adding any other hand-drawn illustrations. Drawing over the grid paper lines is difficult and generally doesn't turn out well.

5. Now you have a good idea of what your project is going to look like. Go ahead and add all the extra finishing touches. Small doodles or even simple dots or squares can really "warm up" the page and keep it from looking choppy.

6. Make your final copies of the page. Easy!

Hints

* Keep a 1-inch (2.54 cm) margin on all edges of your paper.
* If the edges of the cutout pieces are visible on your copies, lighten the copy machine one notch or use correction fluid on one copy and then use it to make the final copies.
* Removable tape is great for creating layouts if you will be using the design more than once.

Clip Art Images on CD

Clip art images presented in black and white in this book are available in both black and white and color on the enclosed CD. If desired, the images can be easily layered to create journal pages. The CD is Mac and PC compatible and requires an operating system of Windows 95/ Mac 8.6 or higher.

Have fun! You can become an artist and create wonderful projects for your class with the help of this book!

December

Bear Tags

5

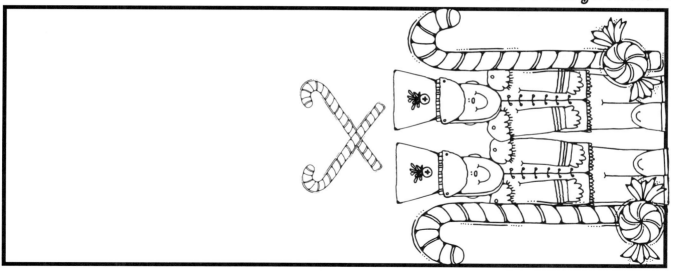

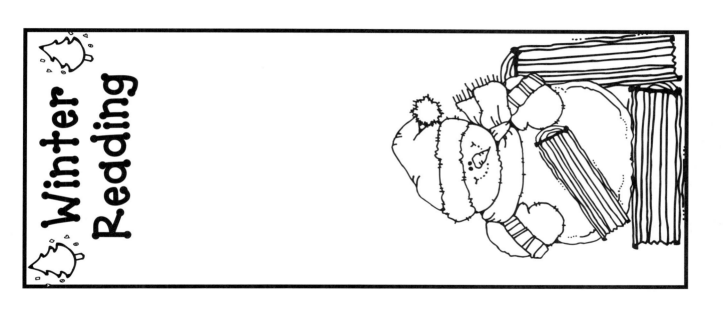

Winter Reading

December Classroom Helpers

just for you!

just for you!

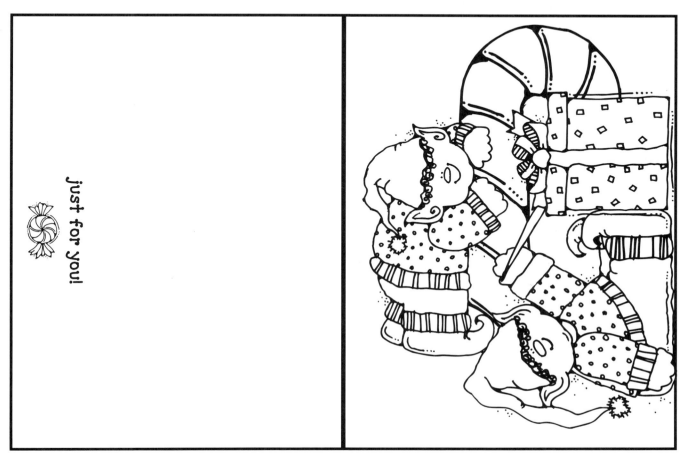

Happy Holidays

Joy

"Bah, humbug!"

Peace

Happy Holly Days

Season's Greetings

Greetings from your teacher

Holiday Happiness

Christmas Cheer

A Season for Giving

Santa Fun

HO HO HO

"Making a list...
checking it twice!"

No peekin'!

Just for YOU!

'Tis
the
Season

14

A note to parents...

Happy Hanukkah

Happy Hanukkah

Festival of Lights

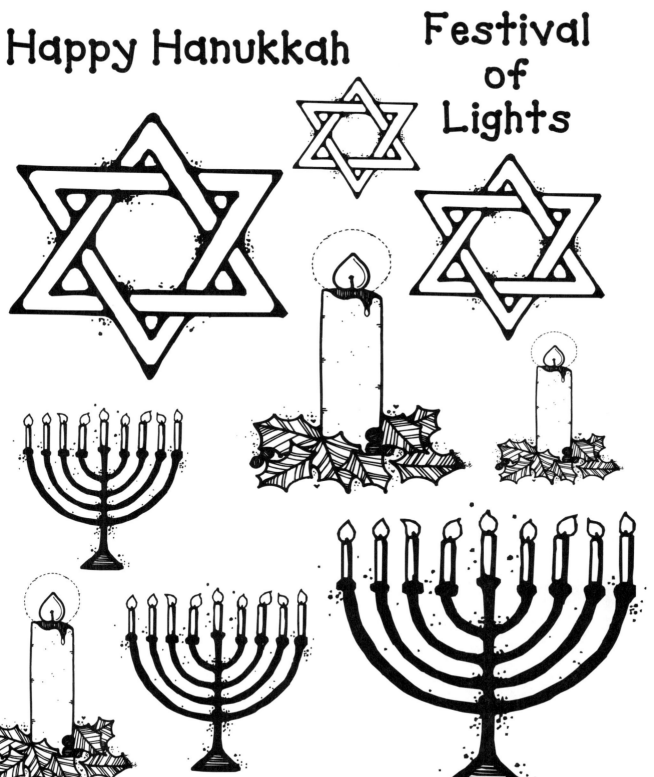

17

Gingerbread Folks

20

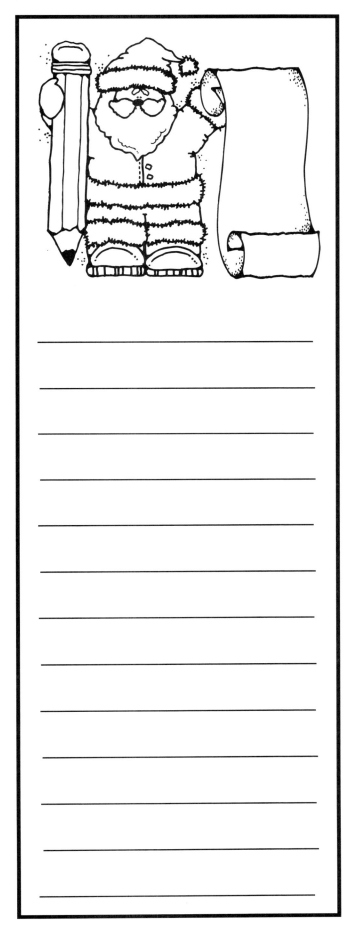

_____

_____

_____

_____

_____

_____

_____

_____

_____

_____

_____

_____

Dear Santa,

December News

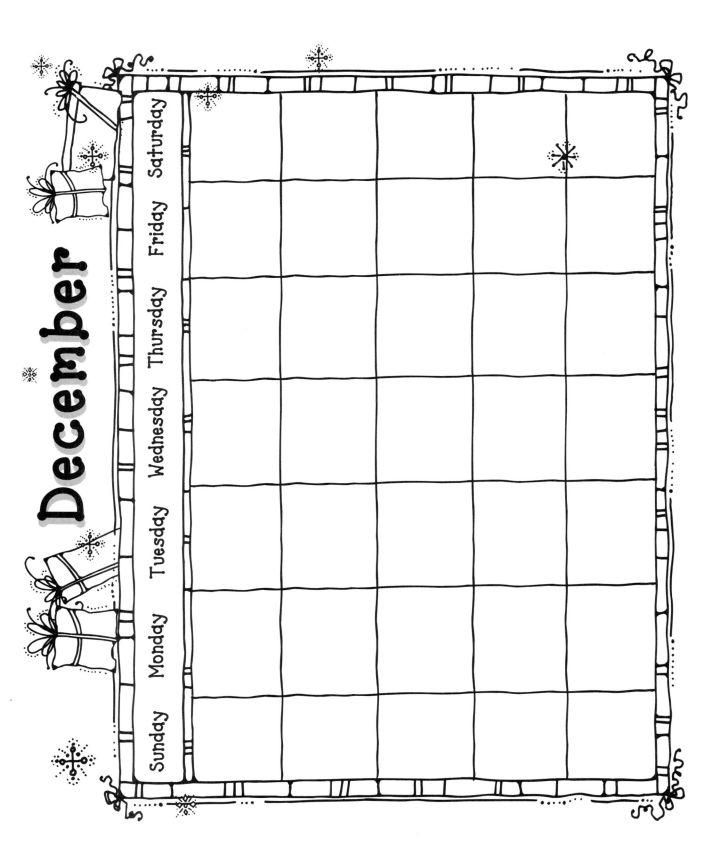

January

Hooray for YOU!

January Birthday List

Brrr! It's COLD!

Snowflakes and Smiles

Happy New Year!

YOU did it!

Great big THANKS!

WINTER NEWS

Spelling List

Homework

Hall Pass

Library Pass

Student of the Month

CELEBRATE

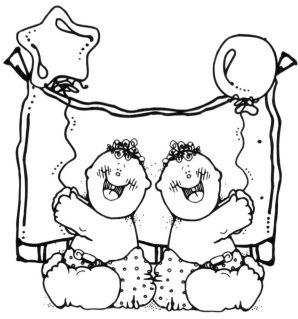

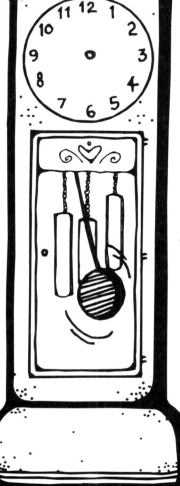

Out with the old...
in with the new!

My
resolutions...

Our class is COOL!

Warm toes and tummies

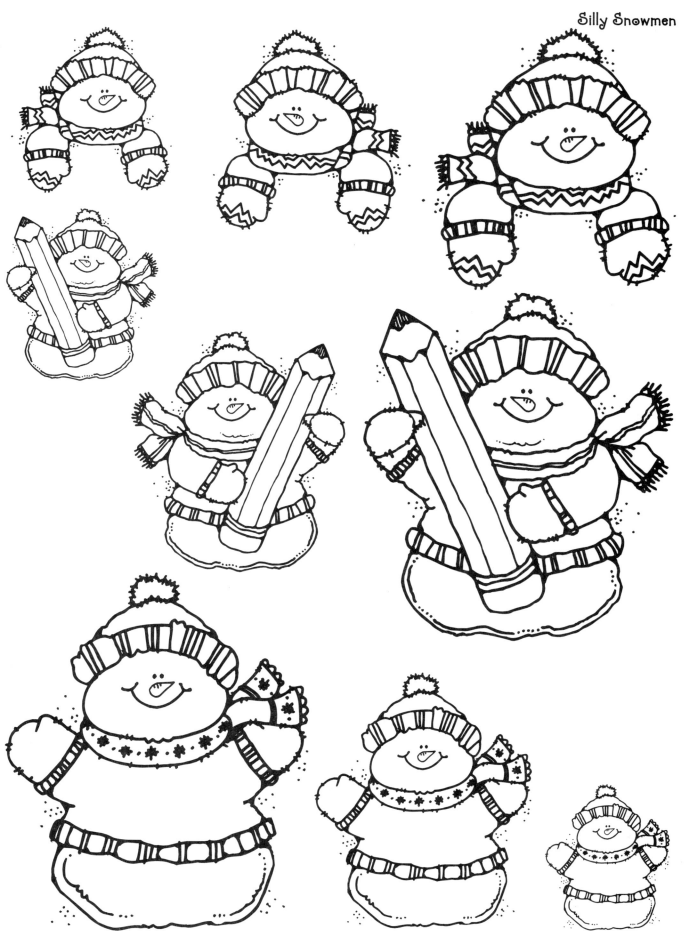

Winter

Happy New Year!

NEWS!

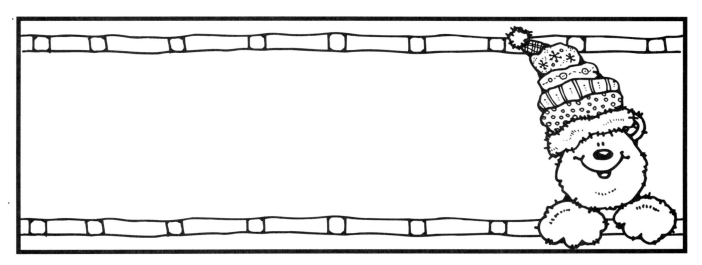

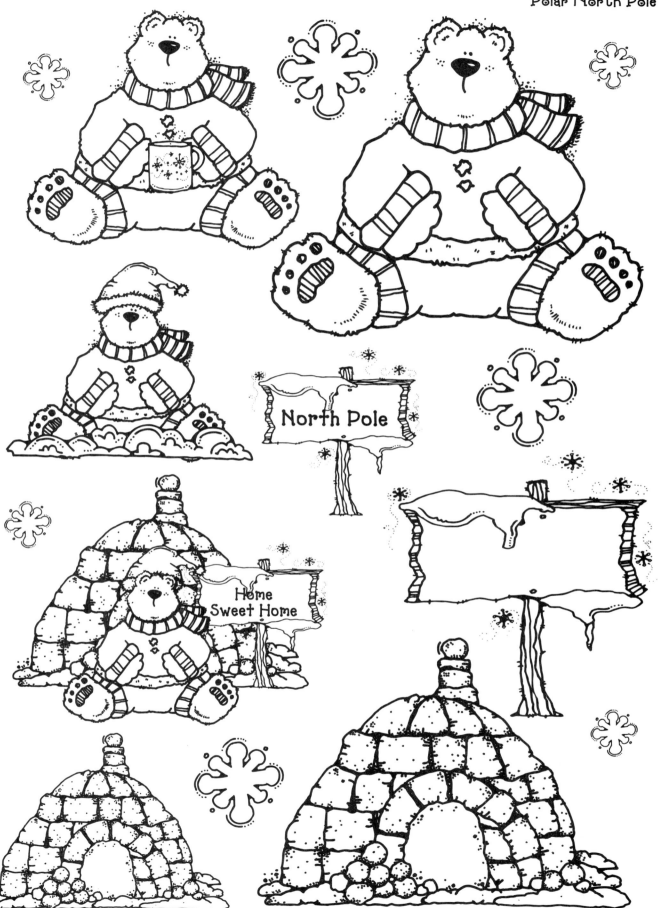

North Pole

Home
Sweet Home

It's snow time!

LET IT SNOW

January News

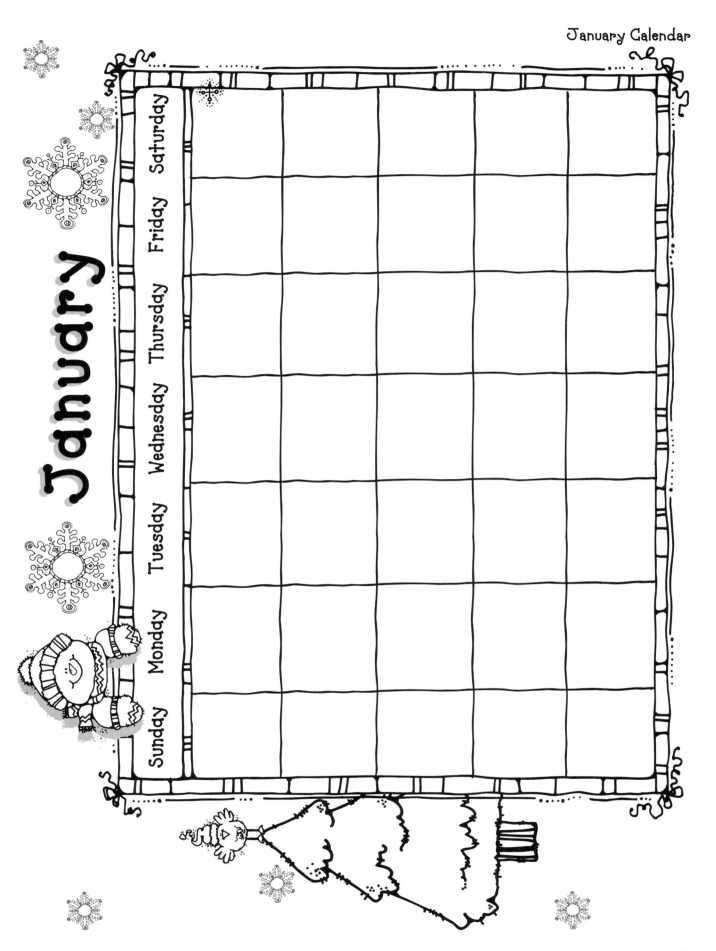

Bake Sale!

Just for you!

Flower Border

48

Be my valentine.

Thinking of YOU!

Valentine's Day Party!

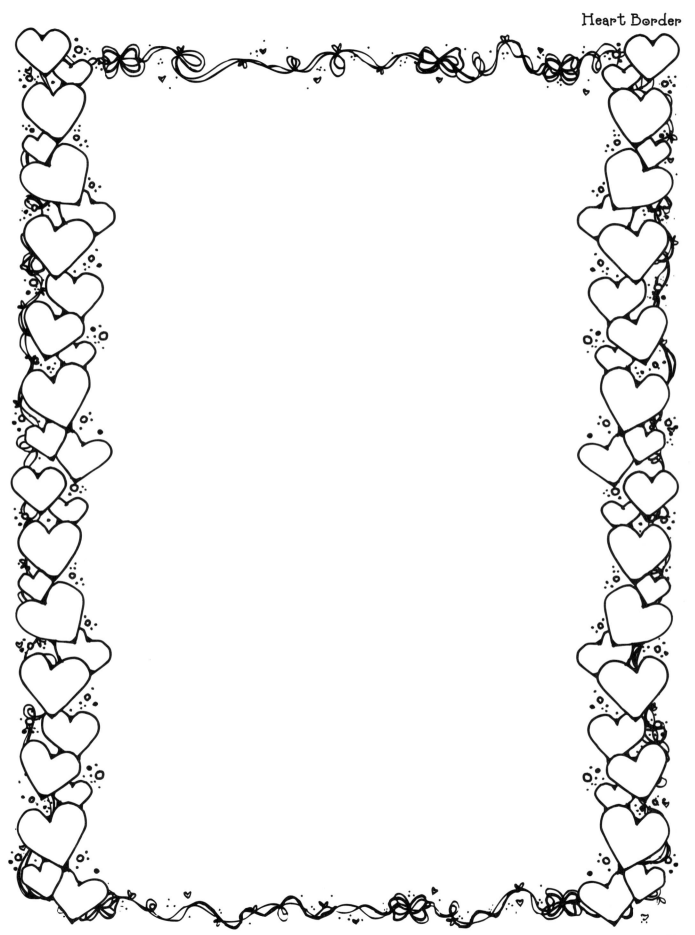

Heart Border

From the
Heart

Just a Note

Thank You

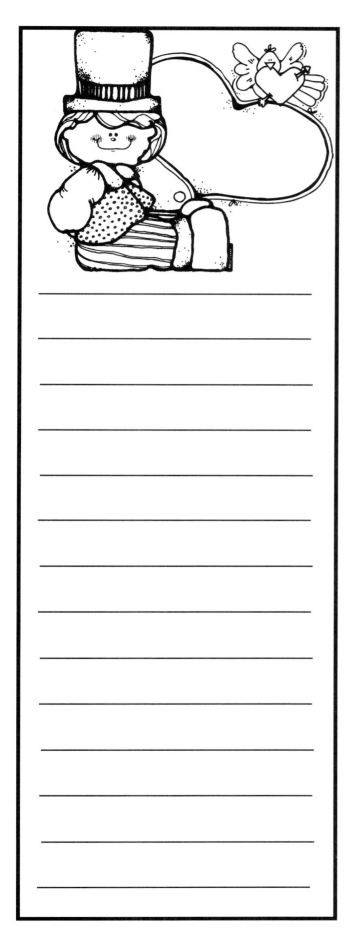

Presidents' Day!

Love Note...

Happy Heart Day!

No "LION," You're the best, Valentine!

Be Mine...

Valentine's Hugs!

You're Special!

February News

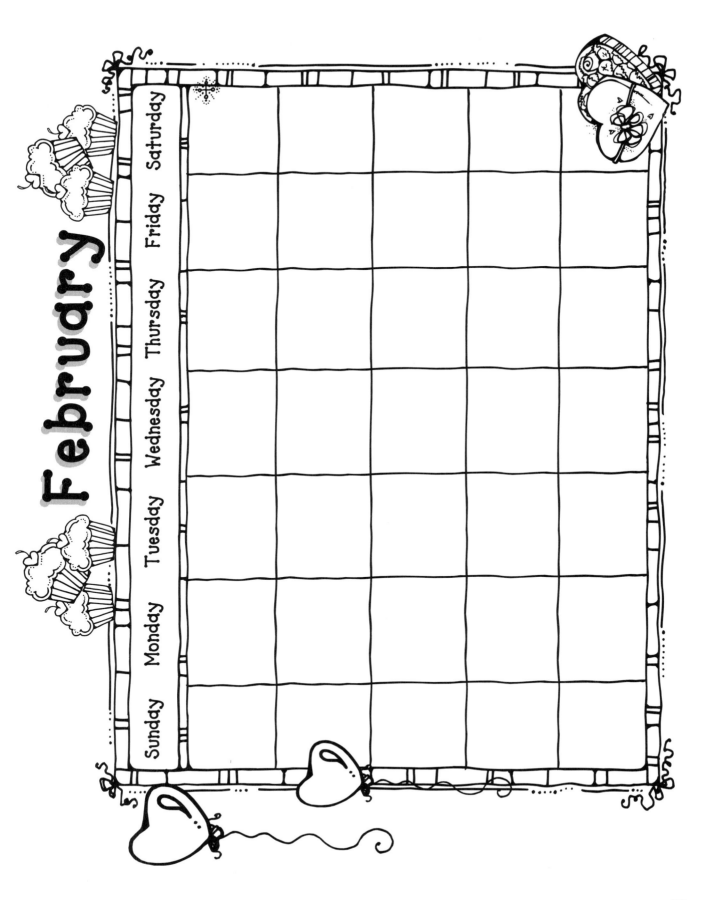

February

Sunday	Monday	Tuesday	Wednesday	Thursday	Friday	Saturday

December

January

February

angeltree   babies   bakesale   balloon   balloonbear   balls   banner   bdaylist   bear2

 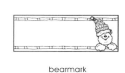   

bear   bearbox2   bearbox3   bearbox   bearbrdr   bearflowers   beargift2   beargift   bearheart

bearlean   bearmark   bearmug   bearpeek   bearsled   bearspocket   beartag2

beartag   bearwheart   bearwhearts   bells   bemine2   bemine   bigthanks   birdbooks

birdy   bow   bowbear   box   butterfly   candelabra (menorah)   candle   candy

candybear   candycane   candycanebear   candytag   canetag   catleaf   catnmouse   celebrate

cheer   cherries   chocolates   classcool   clock   cloud   confetti   cookielist   cookiepals

cookies   cookietag   cupcake   dearsanta   deccalendar   december2   december   decnews

 deertag

 dogforyou

 doggift

 dogheart

 dogsheart

 elf2

 elf3

 elf

 elfcard

 elfgift

 elftag

 fathers

 fathertime

 feb

 febcalendar

 febnews

 february2

 festival

 floralrow

 flowermark

 flowerpage

 flowers

 flowsvase

 flowvase

 foundfather

 fromtheheart

gardenbear

 gardenlist

 garland

gingerhouse

 giving

 greetings2

 greetings

 hallpass

 hanukkah

 happiness

 happyhanukkah

 happyheart

 happynewyear

 happyyear

 hatsbear

heart1

 heart

 heartballoon

 heartflakes

 heartflower

 heartgarden

heartlist

heartmark

heartpage

heartrow

hearts

heartsbear

 hecookie

 helpers

 hholidays

 hnewyear

Ho Ho Ho

hohoho

 holly2

 holly3

 holly

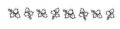 hollybear

 hollydays

 hollyleaf2

 hollyleaf

 hollytag

Homework

homework

 hooray

 hugs

 hugskisses

"Bah Humbug!"
humbug

igloo2

igloo

Burrr! It's COLD!
✻✻✻
itscold

jancalendar

jannews

january2

january

Joy
joy

justanote

Just for YOU!
justforyou

kidswheart2

kidswheart

laceheart

lacehearts

letitsnow

Library Pass
libpass

longballoon

loveballoons

lovebird

lovenote

"Making a list...
Checking it twice!"
making

minitag

mittens2

mittens

money

mouse

mouseballoon

mugs

naturebear

newbabies

newsbear

newyear

nolion

No Peekin'!
nopeekin

North Pole
northpole

Out with the old...
In with the new!
oldnew

opengift

ornaments

P A R T Y
party

partybear

Peace
✻✻✻
peace

penguin2

penguin

penguinflag

penguinlist

penguinpage

penguinsled

pine

pinebear

poinsettia

polarbear

presday

present

president2

president

readmark

reindeer

reindeerrow

My resolutions...
resolutions

Ring the Bells!
ringbells

santa

santadeer

santagift

santahat

santalist

santapen

santatag

63

santawreath   sbearpen   shecookie   sled   smalltag   smiles   snow2   snow

snowball   snowbear2   snowbear   snowbears   snowbird   snowbooks   snowbuds   snowflake1   snowflake2   snowflake3

snowflake4   snowflake5   snowflake   snowflakes   snowhat   snowlist   snowman2   snowman   snowmanpeek

snowmark   snownbear   snowpage   snowpen   snowpile   snowrow   snowsquare

snowtime   snowysign   special   spelling   square   squiggle   star   starballoon   starofdavid

stars2   stars   starsmile   studmonth   tag   tallhat   thankscard   thankyou

thinking   tistheseason   toysoldier   tree2   tree   treemark   trumpet   valentinebear   vase2

vase   vdayparty   walkbear   warmtoes   winbdays   winternews   wintersign   wreath   xmastree   youdidit

© Carson-Dellosa, illustrations © Dianne J. Hook DJ-604011